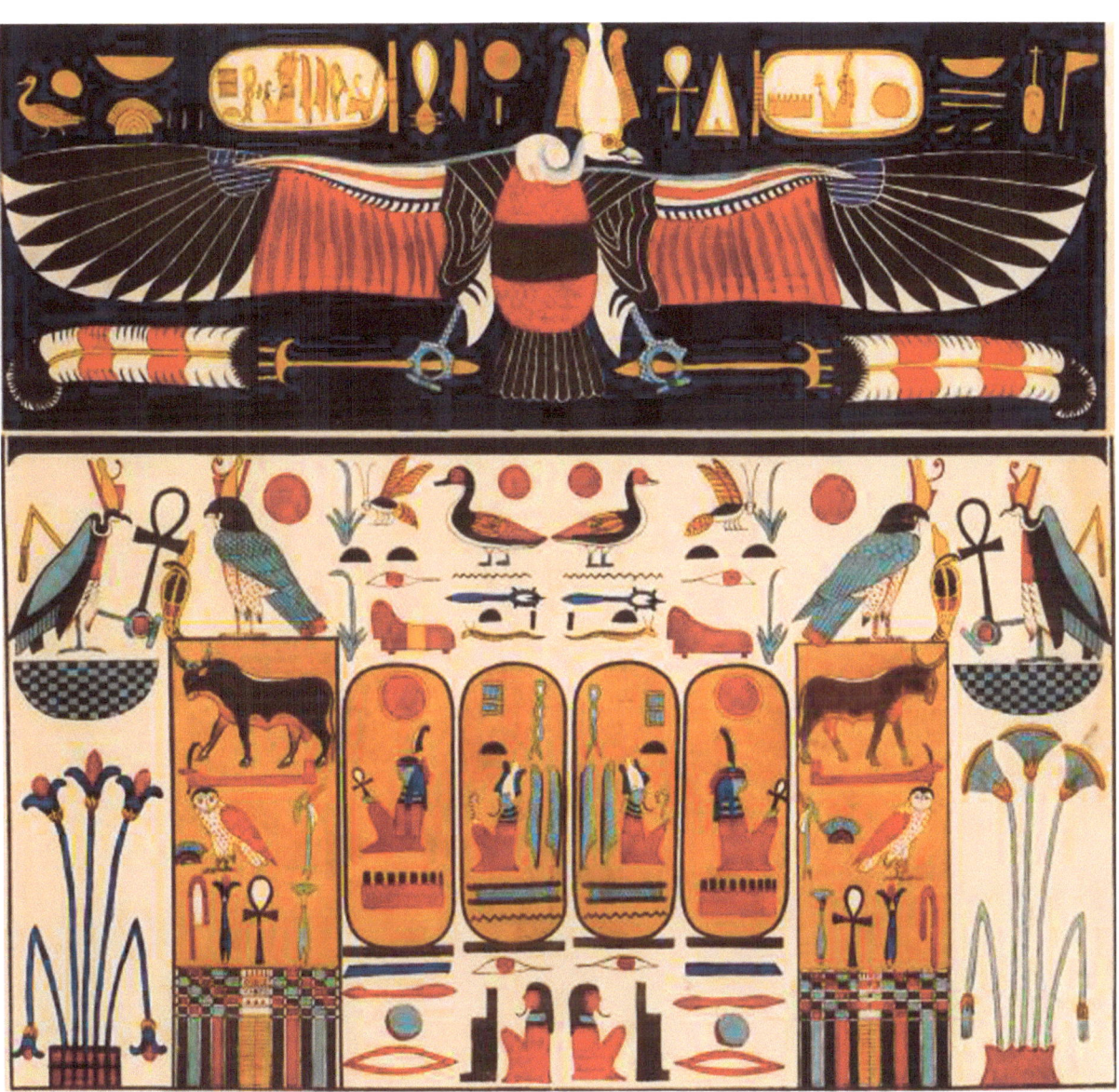

EGYPTIAN PAINTINGS
FROM THE
VALLEY OF THE KINGS

**Paintings on the walls of the once-lost ancient tombs of
Egypt tell many stories of the lives of the Egyptian kings.
When the tombs were rediscovered, researchers
drew copies of the many paintings to keep record of what
they found. The drawings were made into engravings
in 1820, particularly by the engraver J.G.Wilkinson.
His engravings were used as the basis of these coloring pages.**

Coloring book created by Don Landes-McCullogh

Parasol Publishing
1300 SE Park Crest Avenue
Vancouver, WA 98683

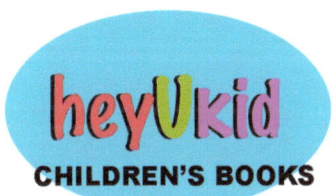

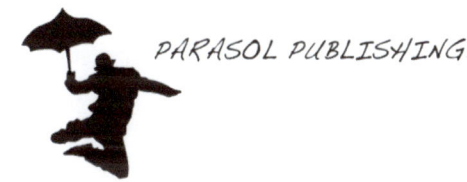

Available through Amazon.com, CreateSpace.com and other retail outlets.

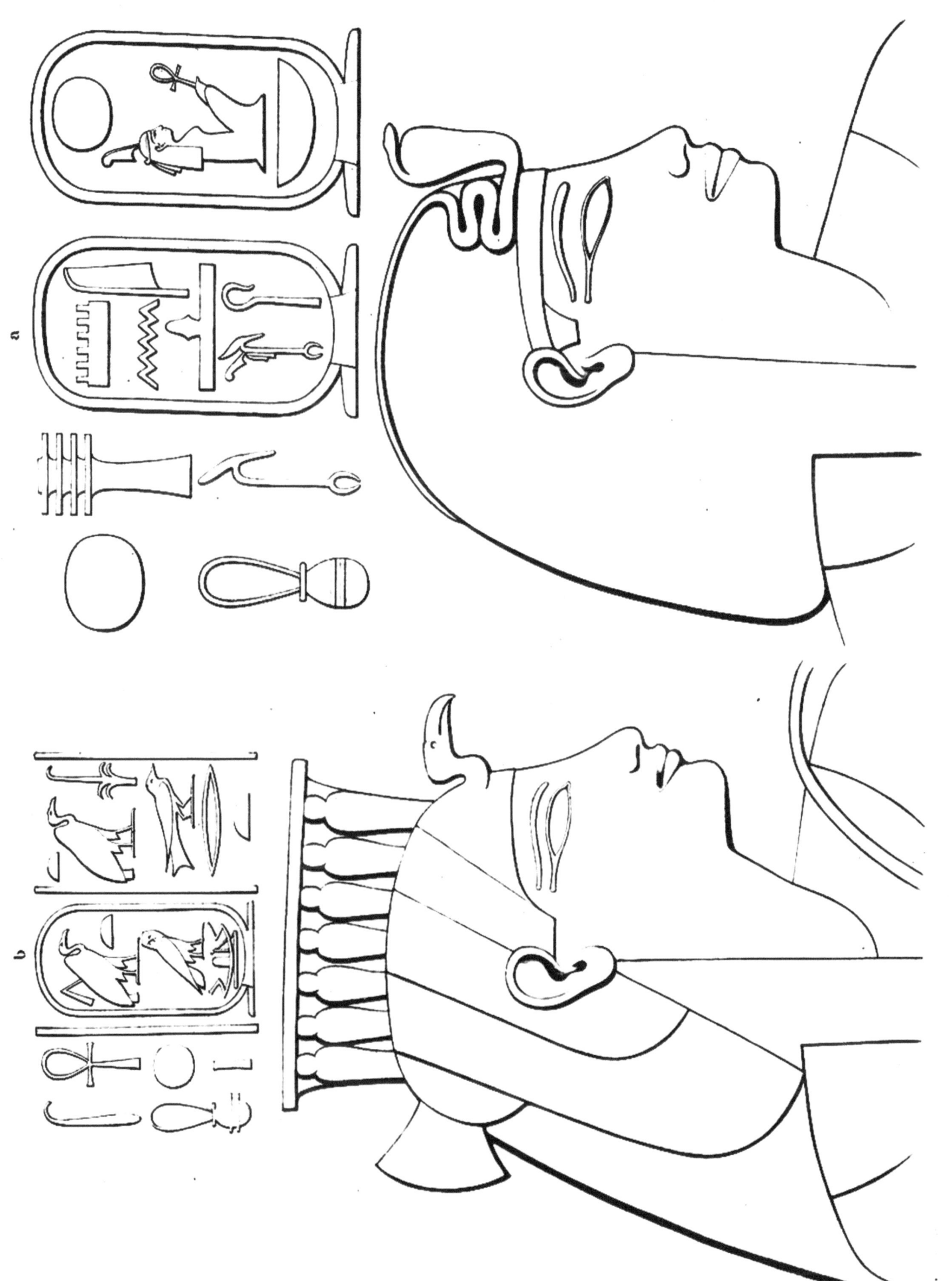

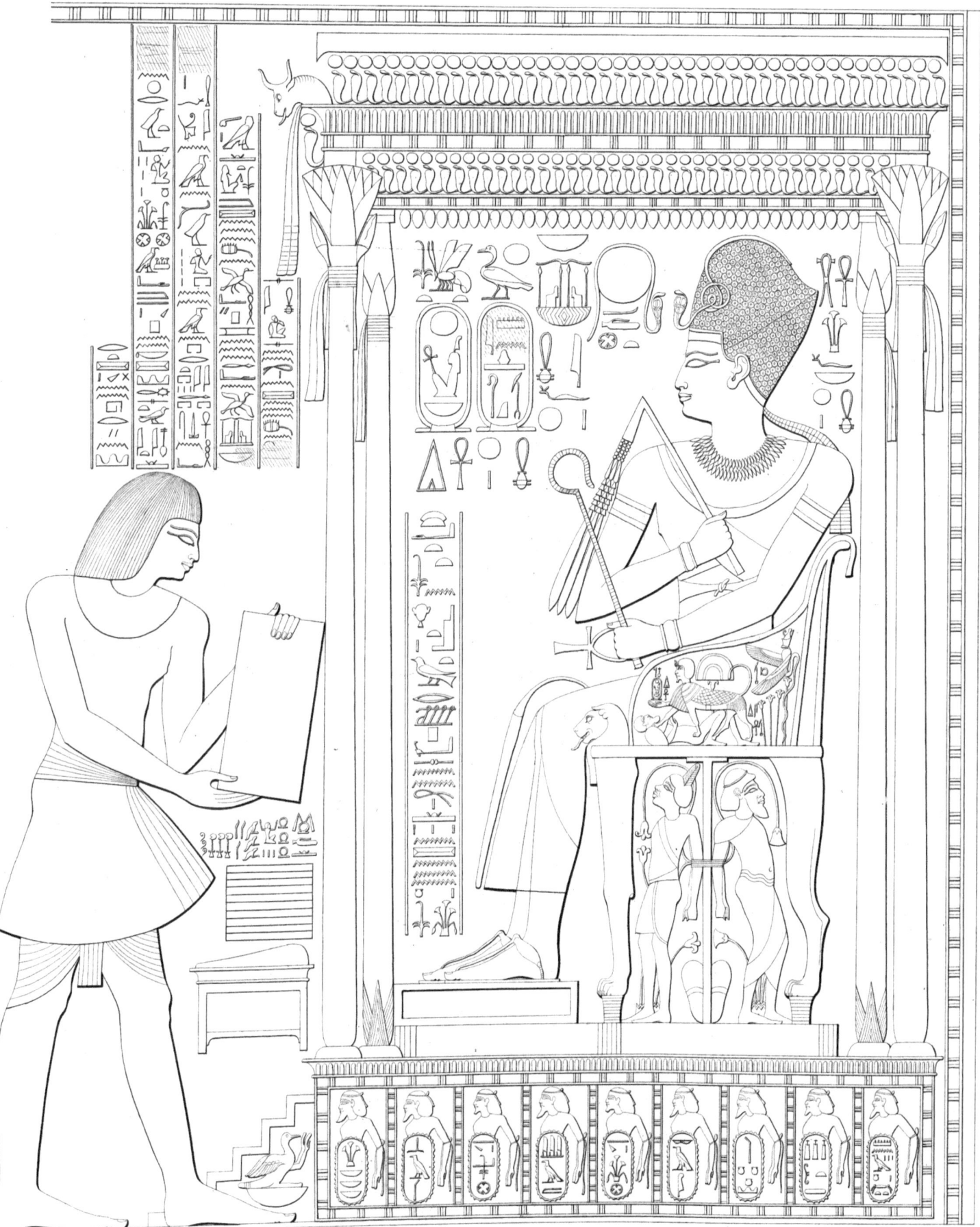

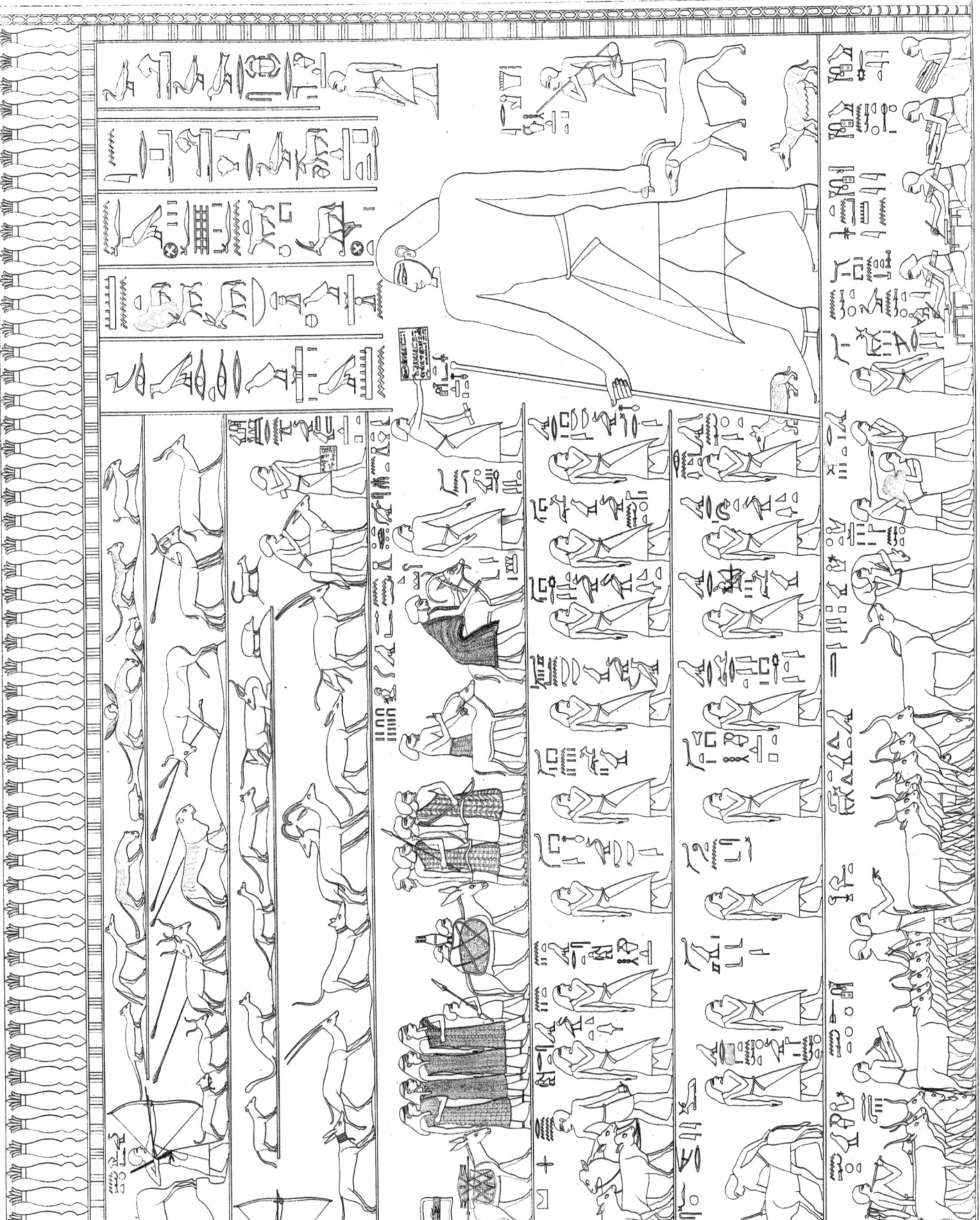

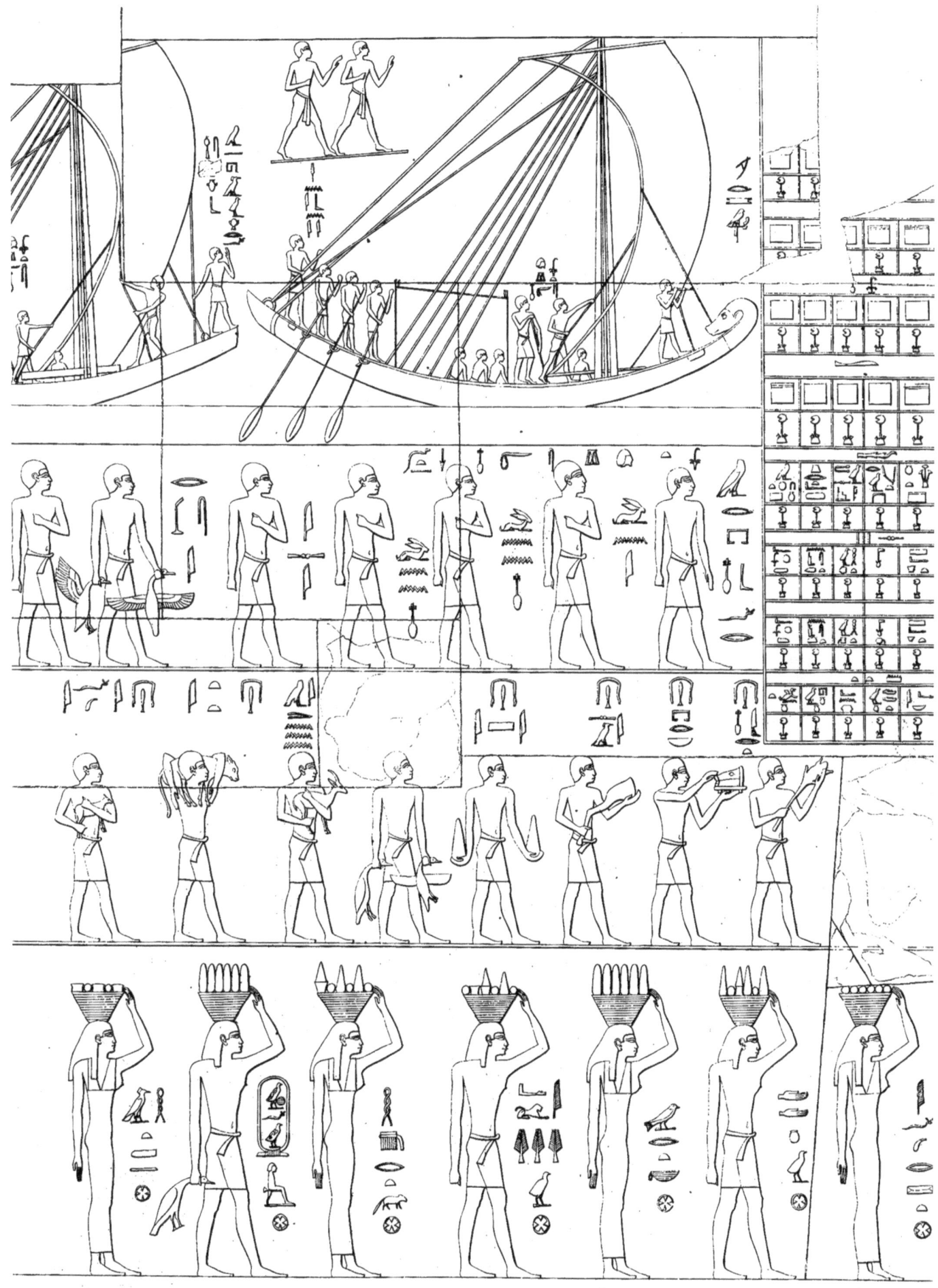

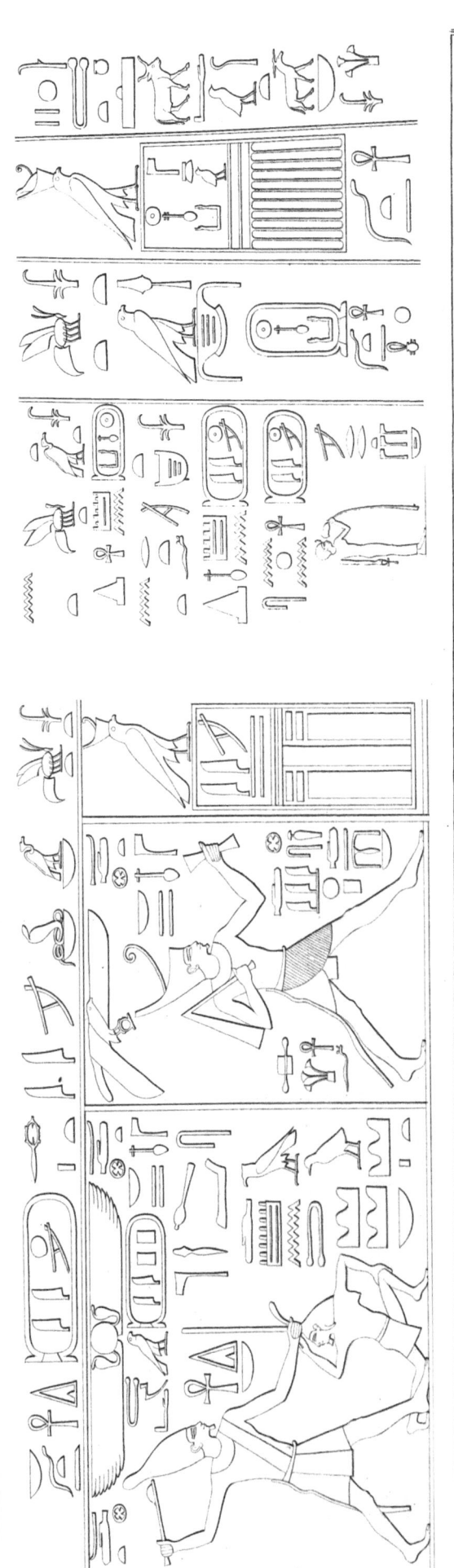

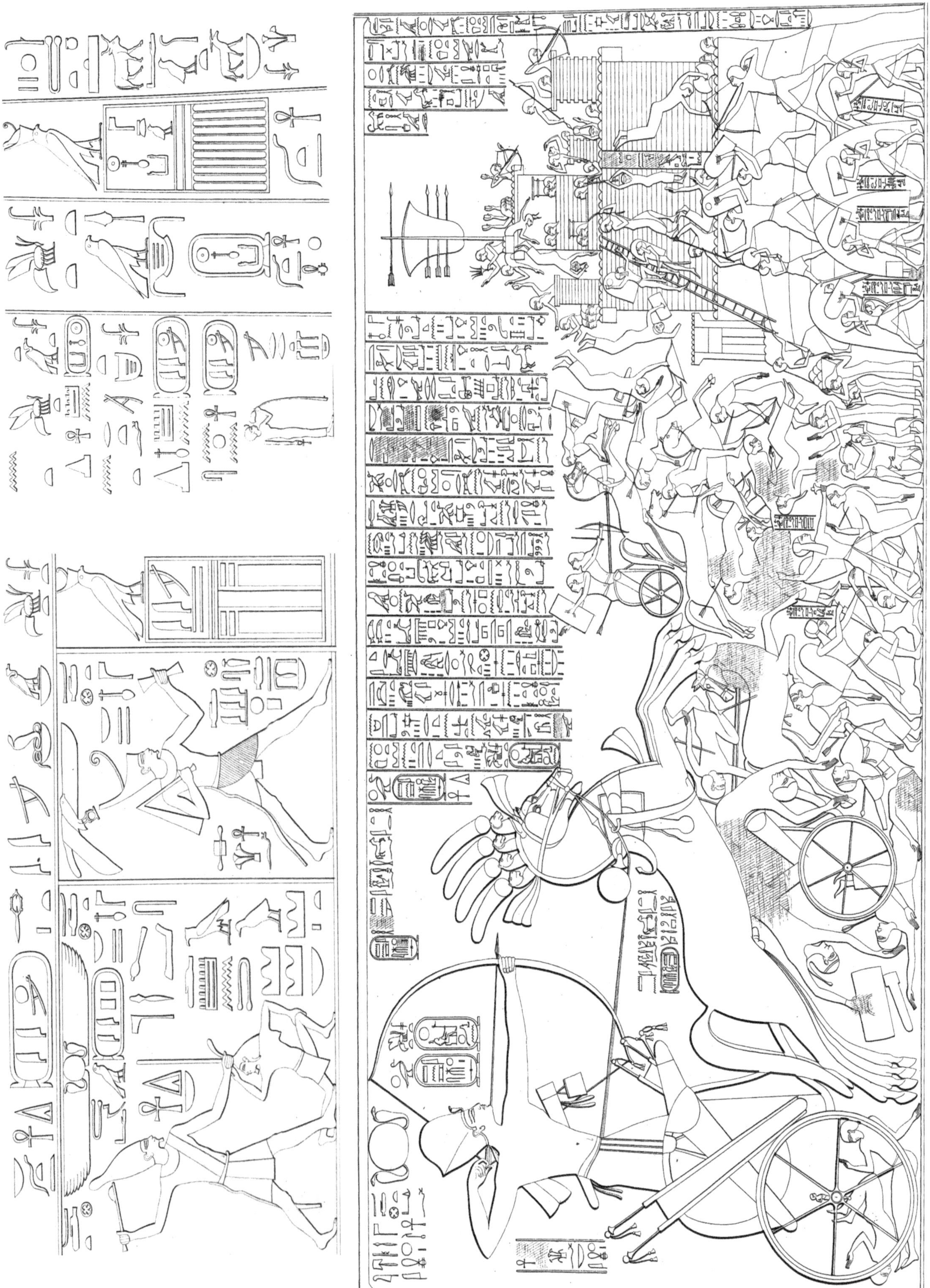

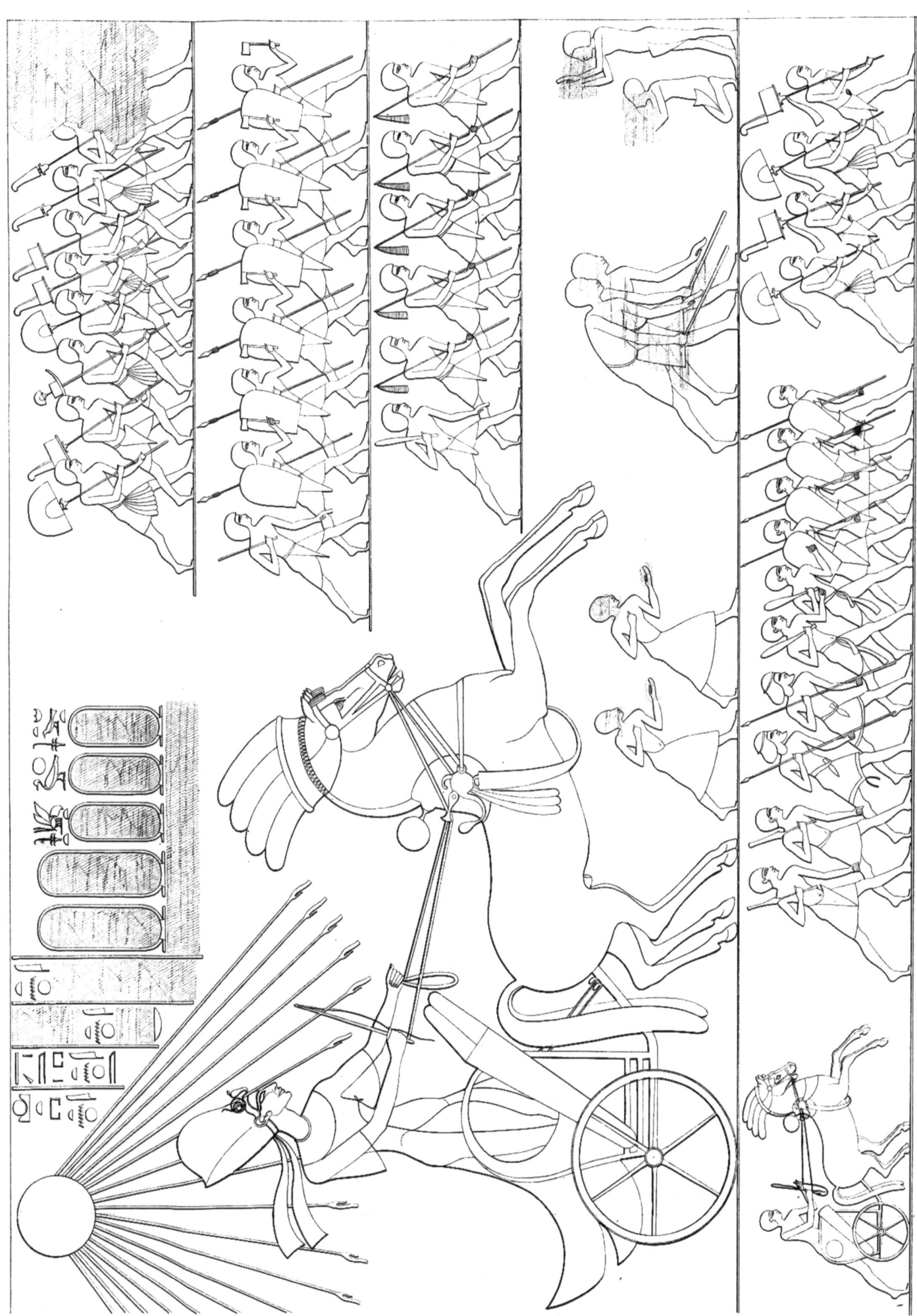

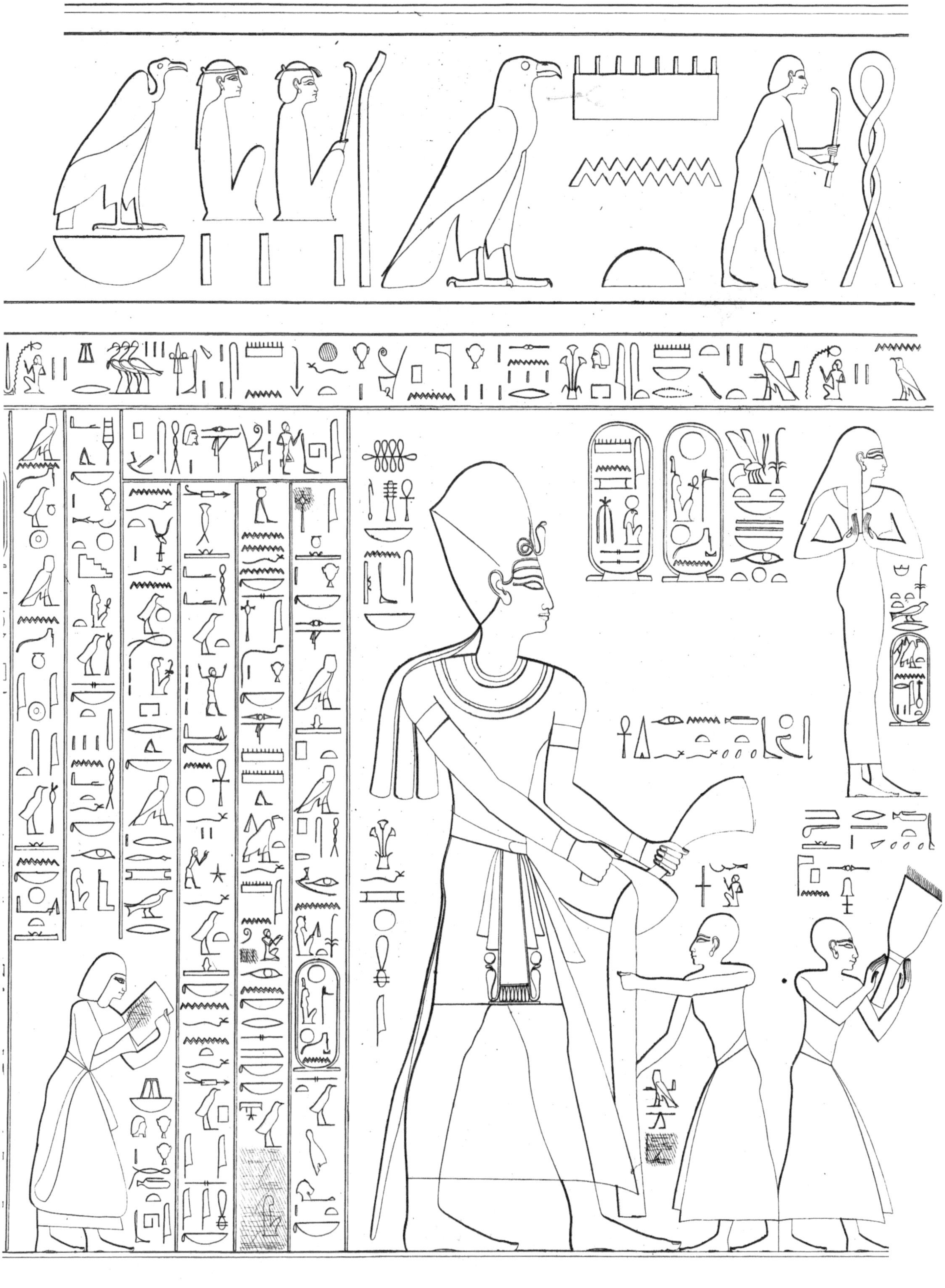

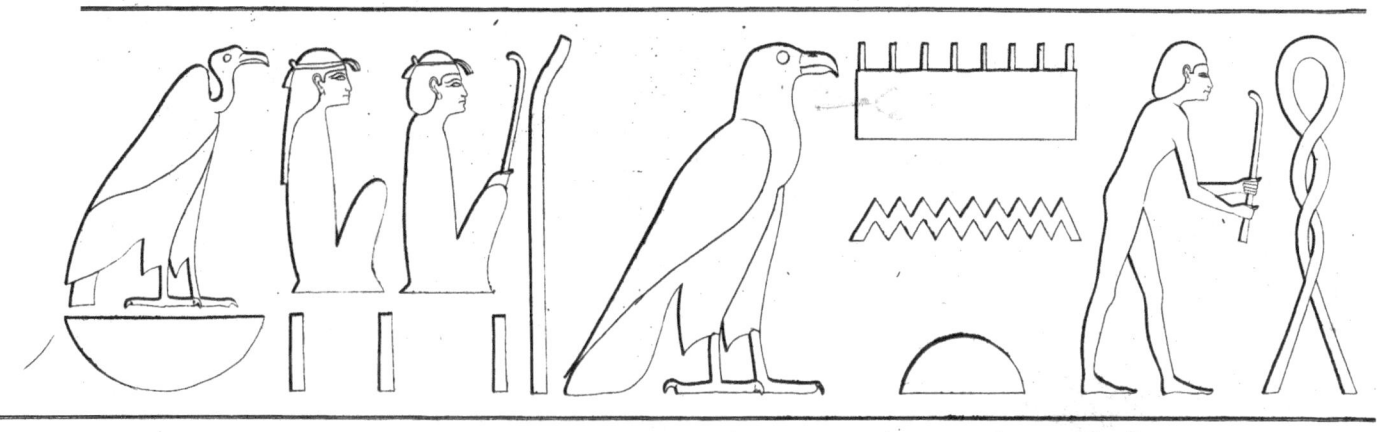

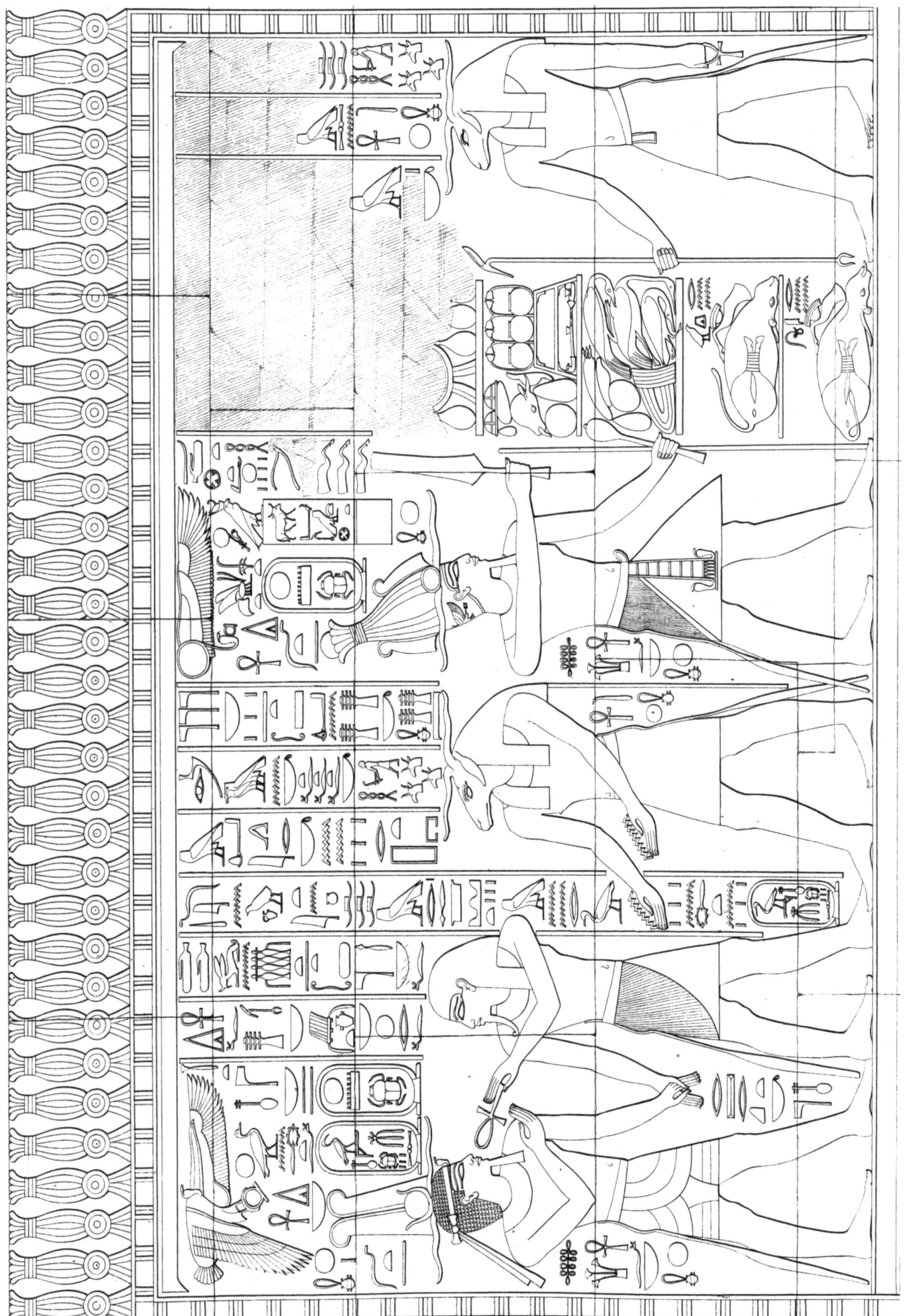

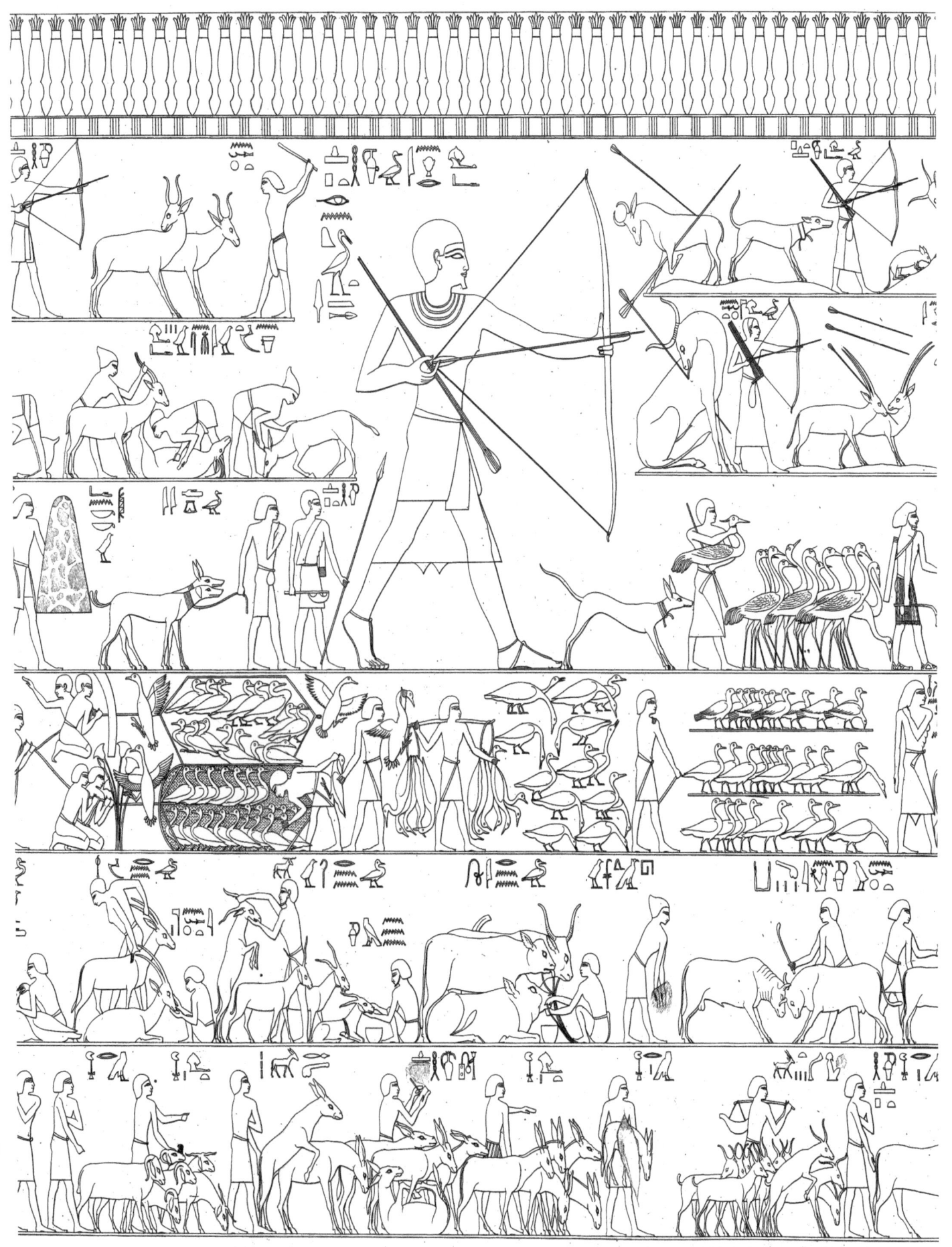

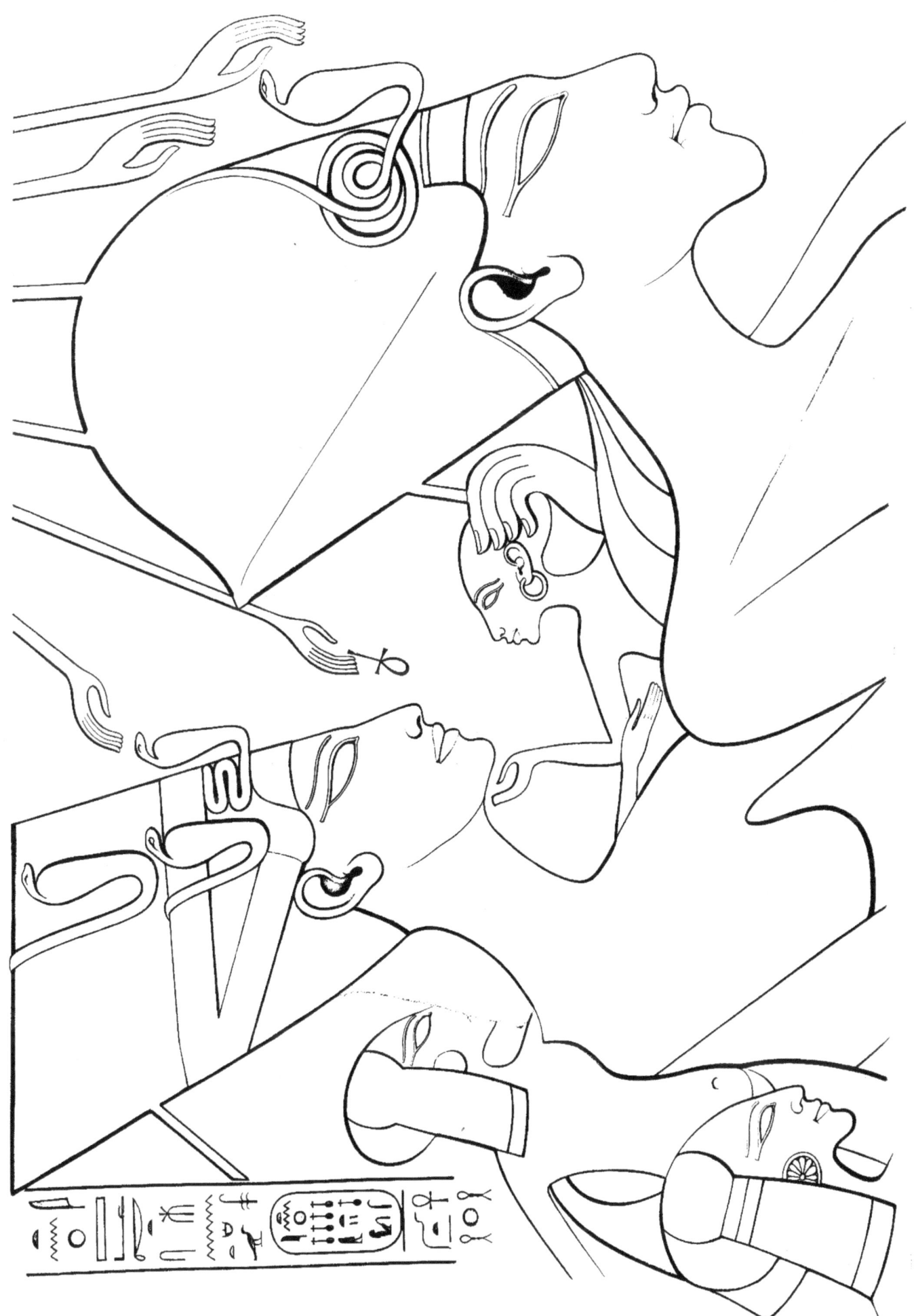

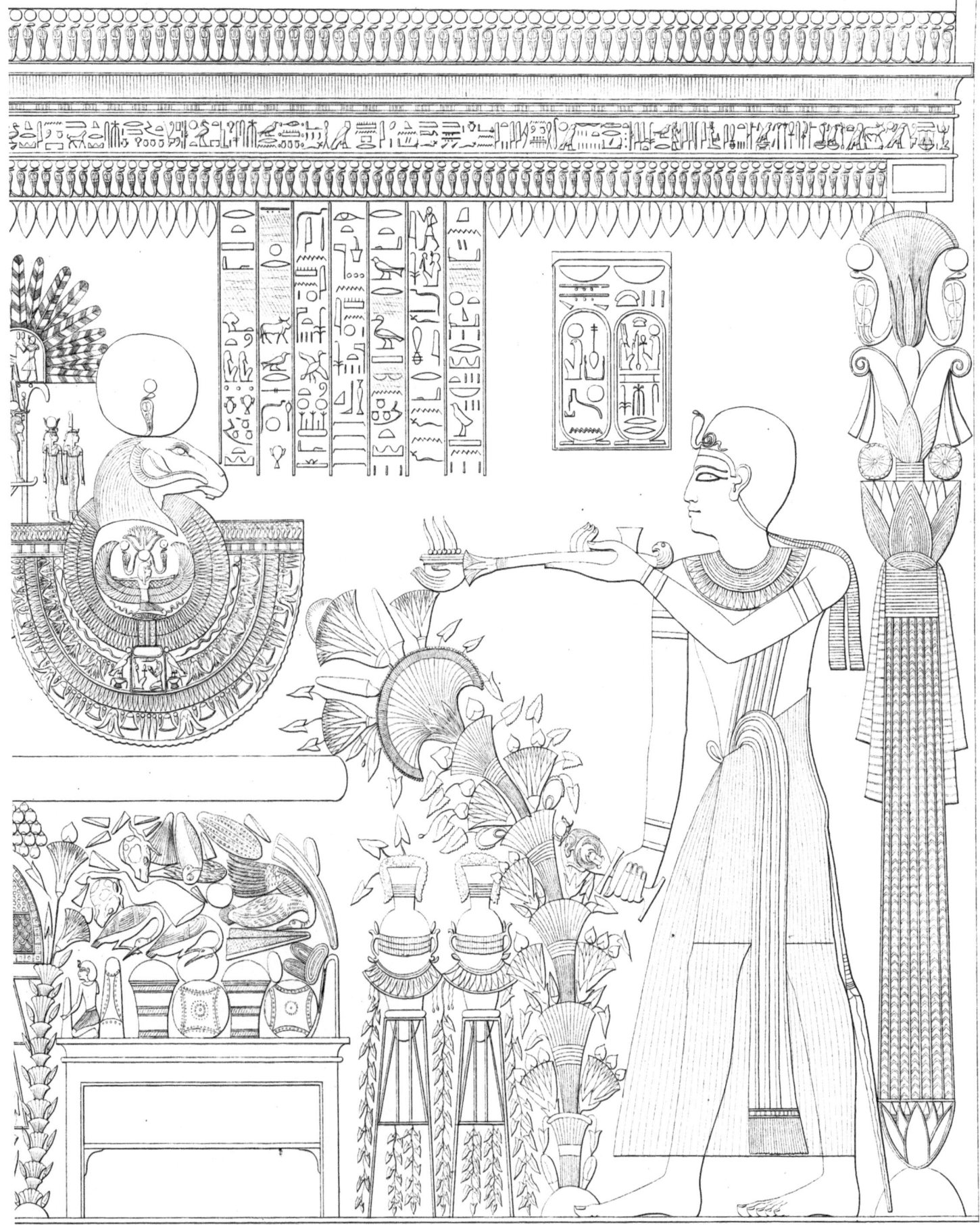

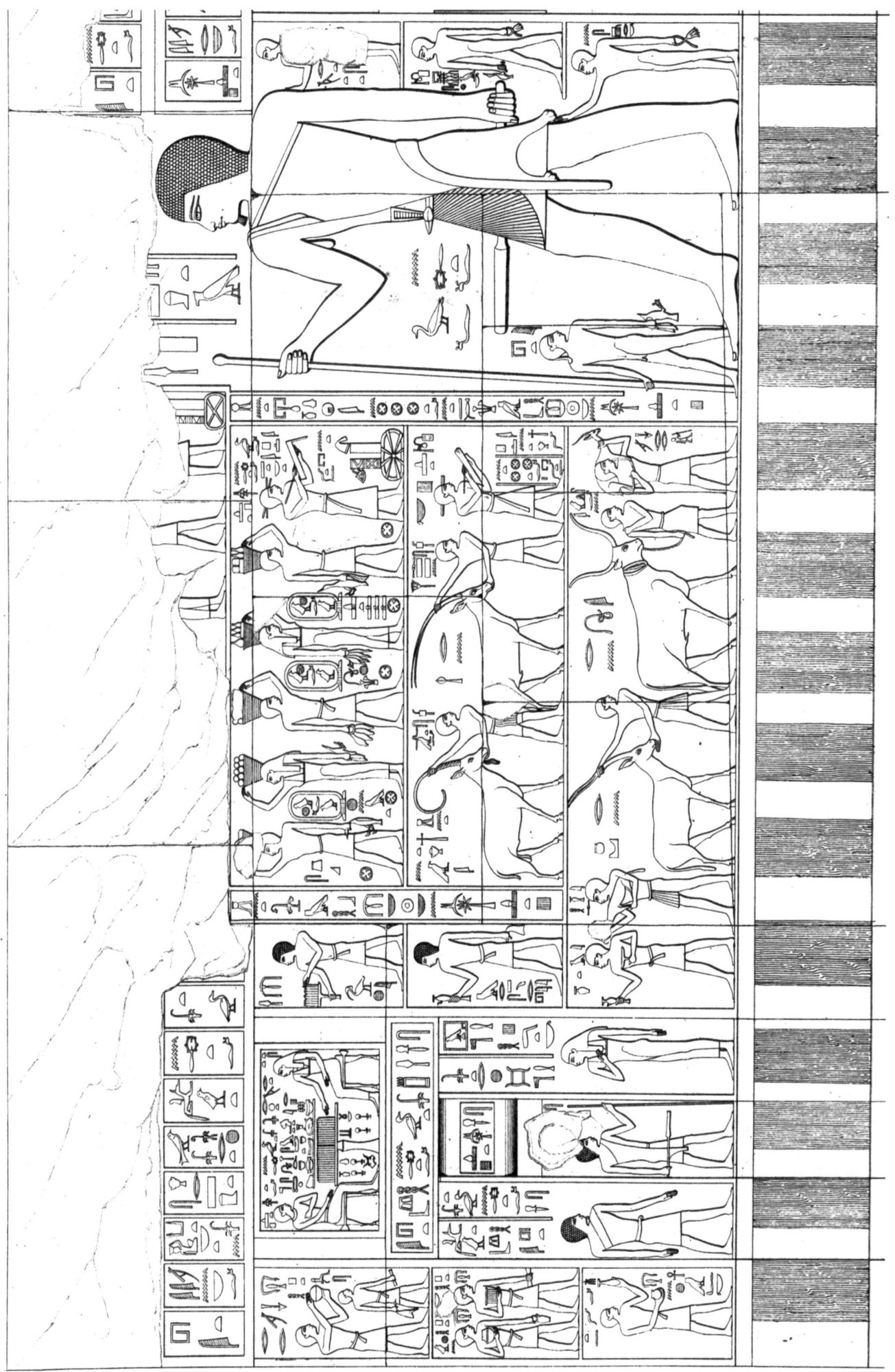

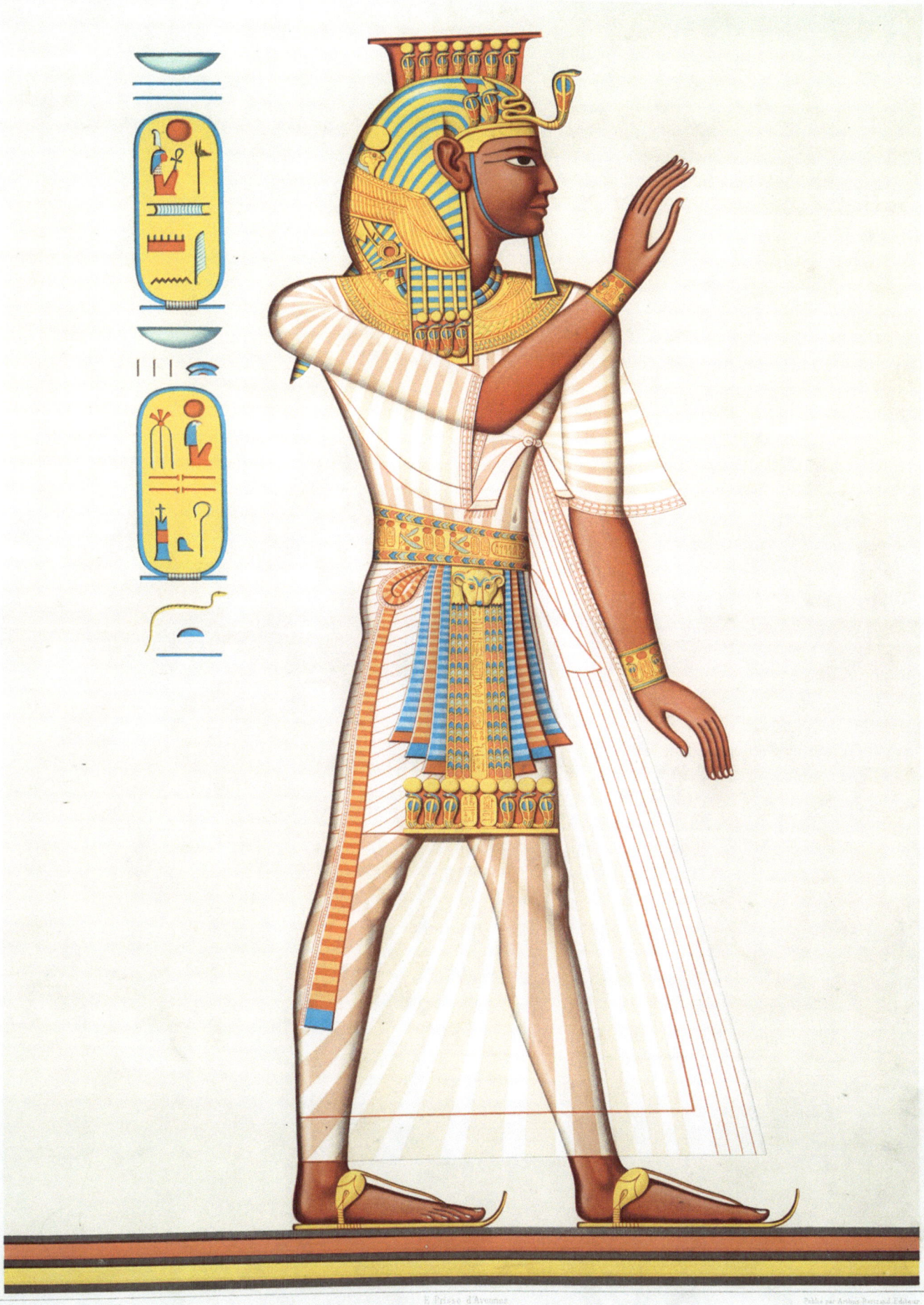

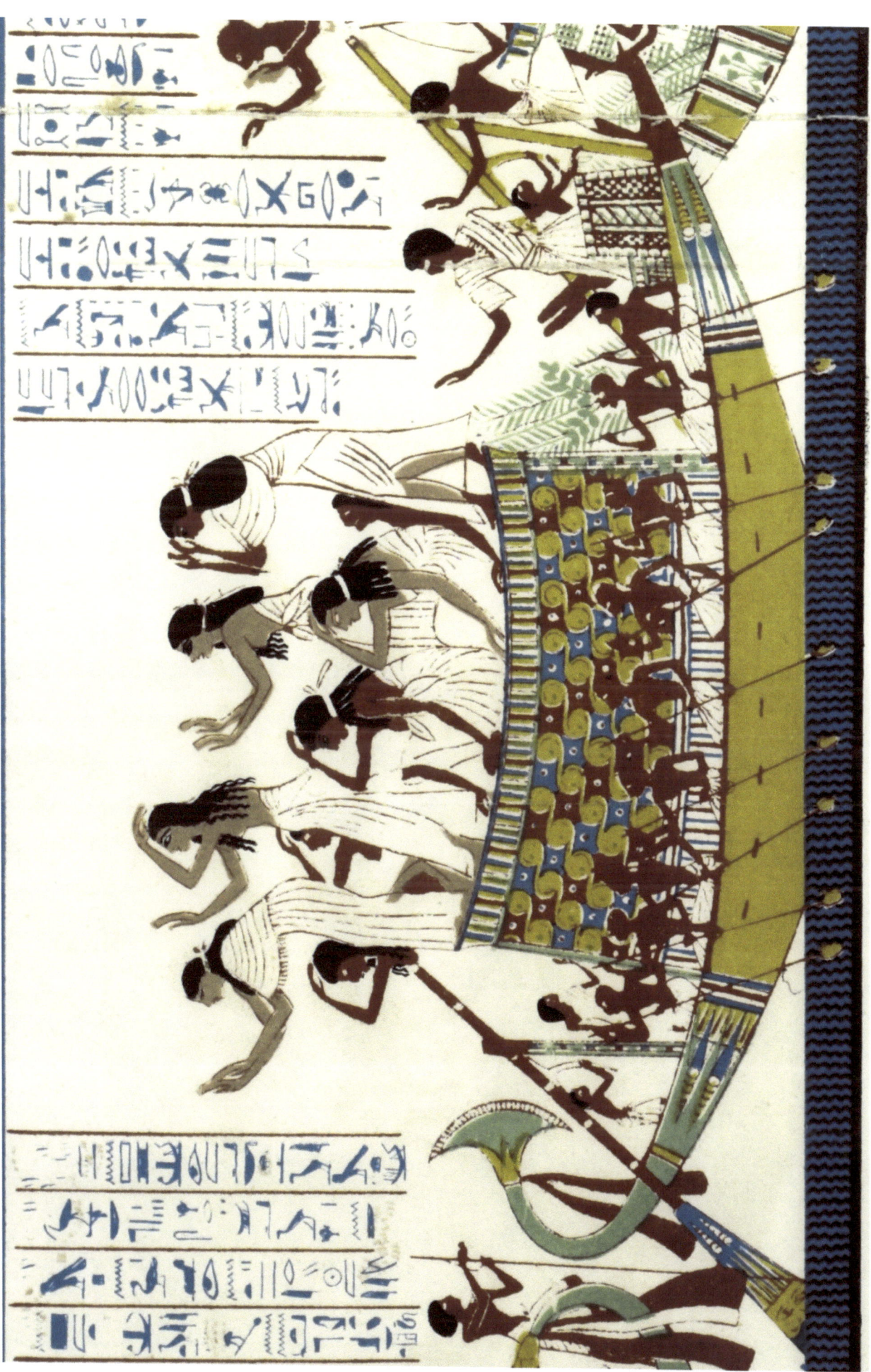

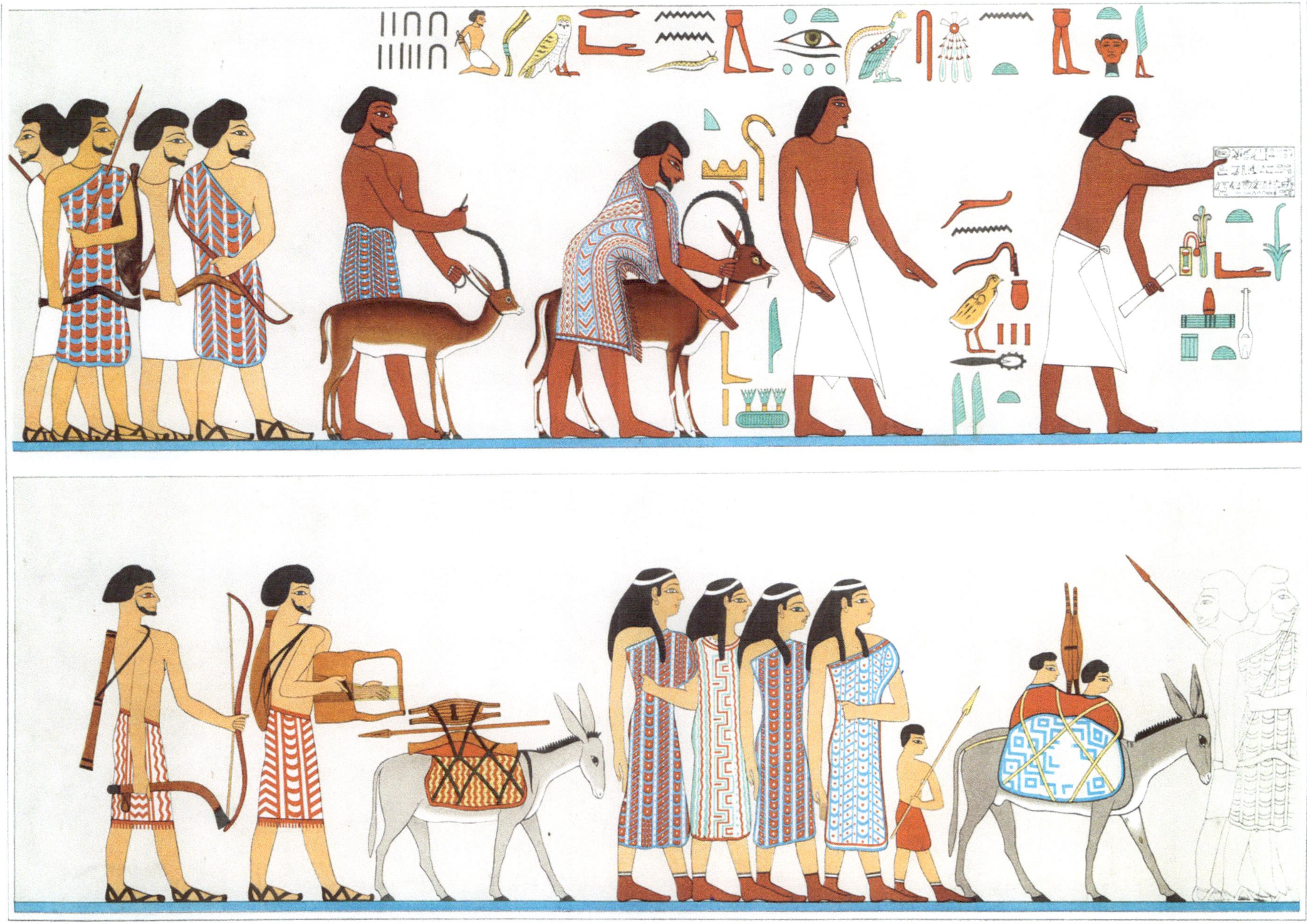

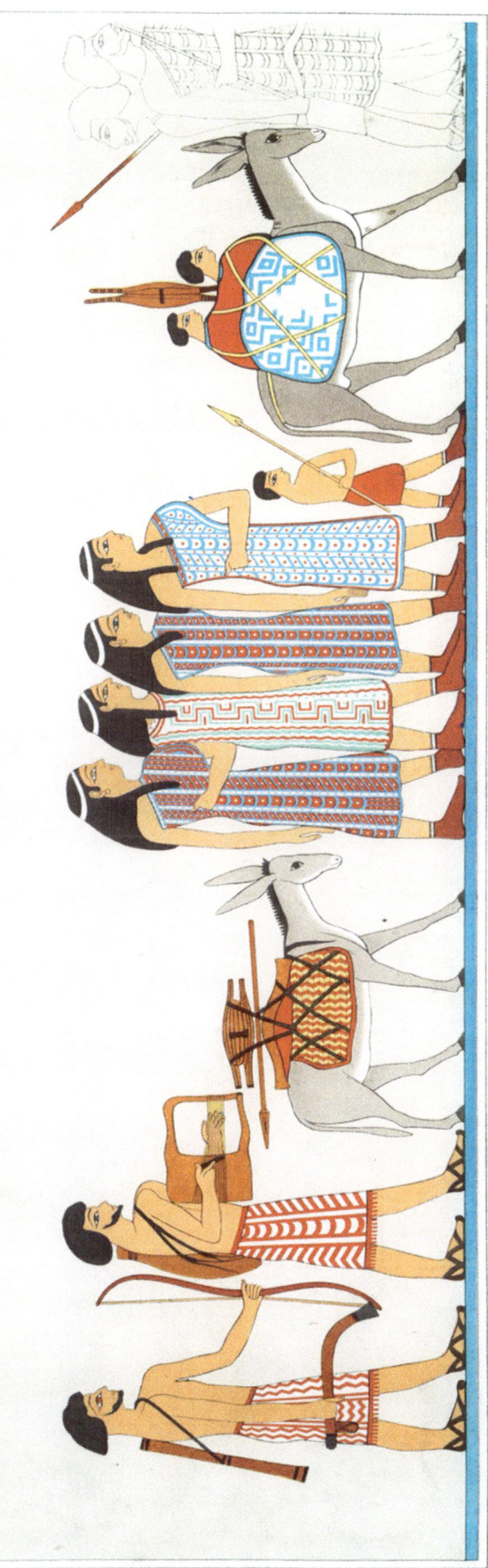

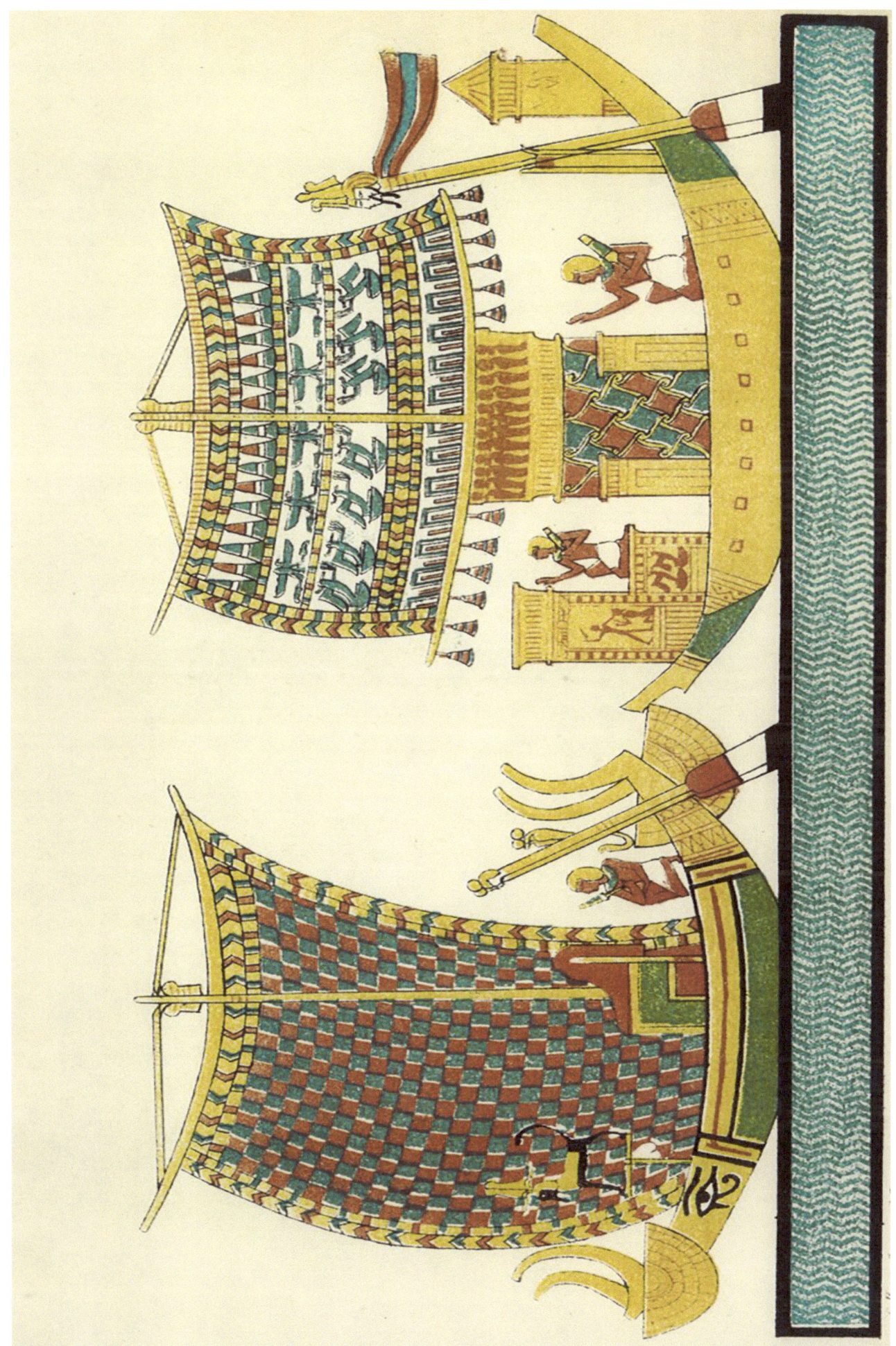

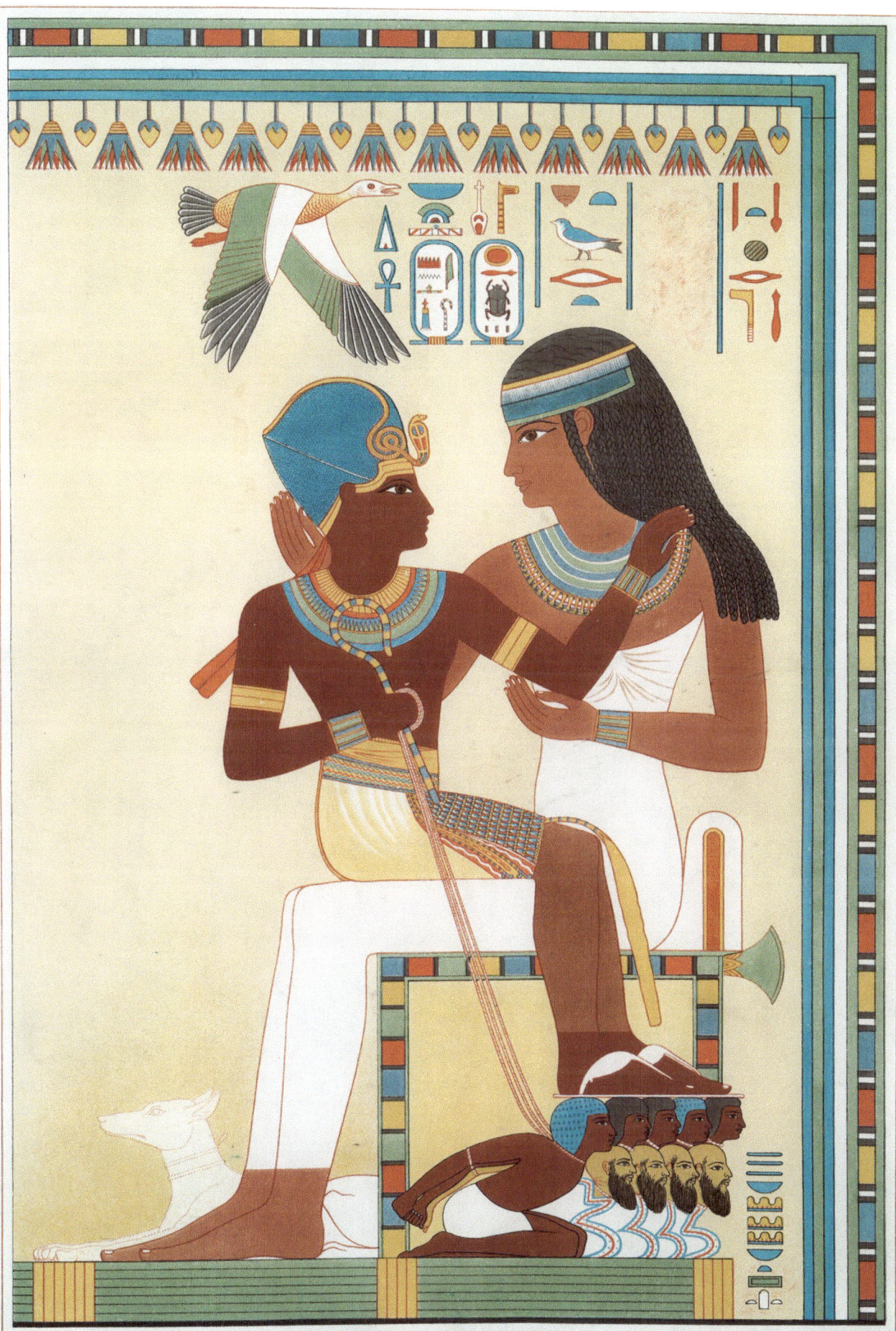